BARE TO MYSELF

BARE TO MYSELF

a collection of poetry by

K. SKY

Dedicated to the child in me,
who was born an artist and
always will be.

TABLE OF CONTENTS

From, The Heart

Moonlit Musings

Preface

Four years ago, my life felt like it had been turned upside down. It was 2020, so I know I'm not alone in experiencing an earth-shattering transformation around that time. I made a choice for myself that I thought I'd never find the courage for. I felt like I had been stripped down to a shell of who I was, which was both painful and liberating. So, I started writing again as a way to return to myself— or really to discover myself for the first time since I was a child.

This collection of poems is a reflection of my life and inner world over these last four years. There isn't one central theme here, just a self-portrait through words; the most unfiltered, unapologetic, and authentic expression of myself. But, we are all reflections of each other so if you are reading this book, maybe you'll find pieces of yourself here too.

So much care and dedication went into this creation. These words needed a place in the world and in the hearts of others. Whether you end up loving these poems or not, this book made its way to you for a reason. I invite you to sink into each page and allow yourself to feel deeply.

The only way out is through.

Dancing with My Shadows

K. *Sky*

I

If roots grow down
Through water and mud,
And some flowers only bloom
With the moon,
Then I too can grow
In ways no one else understands.

II

What is that feeling?
Can you describe it to me?
Is it like walking through a park at night
With cozy streetlights?
Mysterious but comforting,
Charming and familiar,
With an alluring invitation for romance.

How deep is it?
How intense?
Is it like being carried away
By a massive wave?
Or like being pushed onto shore?
Finally able to breathe.

And why don't I know?
Where has it been?
Did it come and go without me knowing?
Or is it always there, has it always been?
Am I simultaneously running from it as I search?
Is it also seeking me?

I'm out of analogies
Because its qualities elude me.
I just really want to know,
Where did that feeling go?

III

I mirror mountains
Oceans, vines, and clouds;
Echoing physicality
With feeling.

Rocky ledges of uncertainty
Before peaks & valleys,
Deep wells of unknowns
That I carry until they're too heavy,
Just to retrace what I release.
Eternally climbing, sprawling
To explore every surface—
      Roots only let me get so far.

I'm a pool of pleasure,
An avalanche of emotion,
Essence of the universe
Experiencing herself.

At the core there is matter
Atoms & structure.
At the core there is consciousness
The soul & self.
And it's all the same
And entirely different.

IV

I like to keep all the memories
Of the past
And the pain.

There's not a moment of my life
I would want to forget
Despite any disgust or regret.

I'll mourn the time that I can't get back
When I lost the possibility
Of who I could have been.

But not even for a second
Would I change
What I've done or who I am.

V

ALCHEMY

It felt like drowning
And burning
At the same time.

I had been broken
Carved into & changed,
Not of my own accord.

It felt like being stripped of my skin
When I ripped off the bandage
And like seeing light
For the very first time.

It felt like a dark room—
        No sense of direction,
No glimpse of what was
Or what could be,
Completely desolate.

It felt like chaos
Madness & confusion,
Liberating & lonely
Empty space
Waiting to be filled.

Then all of a sudden—
        It felt whole.

Rebuilt with entirely new pieces
I had collected.

Out of nowhere, I could breathe,
I could exist in any form I wanted.
It was a garden that took years
To grow
But it felt like a light switch.

Without even realizing it,
I had healed.

VI

THE MOON XVIII

Shutting it out
Won't make it go away—
    That intuitive feeling.
Redirecting the blame
Won't change the truth.

When your heart is lit on fire
Or your stomach sinks
Or your throat constricts
Listen—
    Because resisting your intuition
Long enough
Does damage.
You have to reintegrate
Relearn how to trust yourself
To distinguish between triggers & guidance.

If you were looking for a sign
This is it—
    I promise there is life after this.

VII

Thoughts consume me
Focused & flooded
I try to shift
To shake free
From the hold
But I'm tethered
Tied up & bound
With barbed wire—
    Pain laced with pleasure
Feels better
Than feeling nothing at all.

VIII

Disconnect
Disconnect me
Disconnected
From what feeds & fuels me
Nothing is what it used to be
All pained, put out, and moody
Give me some time
To go find me.

Tested
Rejected
Neglected
This fucked me up
There's nothing left in my cup
I can't seem to fill it
Back up.

Give me back who I was
Or let me be changed
And reclaim my lust
For living.

I can feel myself closing off
Wrapping myself in everything
I've lost
Taking it all in
And at the last moment
I'll pop.

IX

PMDD

It's like I'm locked in a frosted glass case.
No one can see the pain in my eyes or
hear my muffled words.
Surrounded by people who touch the glass and
try to speak to me, but I'm alone in here.
I feel so alone.
It gets dark, like heavy clouds closing in. Violent
winds promise the storm will pass, but there's no
light on the horizon.
So the rain lasts forever.
I can't see out into the world, but I feel the weight of
it pressing down on me.
There are tools at my feet, none of them useful.
I tap and push on any weak spots,
but that glass is impenetrable.
Press my hand against it when someone reaches out
to touch it, but it's cold.
The connection— blocked.
My container drives me insane. I pace in tiny circles,
retracing every inch,
Trying to understand why I ended up here.
Or I collapse and stare out, letting my eyes unfocus
to match the frosted surface.
Repeating, "I can't do this."
I can't do this.
I can't do anything but wait.
For the clouds to part.

For the glass to shatter.
A temporary death sentence.
A prison I know isn't permanent, but feels fatal.

X

I thought I knew myself
Completely
But I don't.

Layers & layers
And layers
To pull back
Like a kaleidoscope
Changing with every turn,
Different each time
I look deeper.

It makes me wonder
If I can trust myself
But I suppose that's
Human nature,
We aren't fixed or stagnant.

Somehow
I'll have to learn
It's okay to change
My mind.
To be someone different
Moment to moment.
To exist completely
Unrestricted.

XI

For personal reasons
I'll be going insane,
Becoming completely delusional;
It's all made up anyway.

For personal reasons
I'll be growing,
Making more mistakes,
Turning into someone you don't know
Because, *god*, I can't stand staying the same.

For personal reasons
I'll be spending more time alone
Because my favorite company
Is my own,
And only I know just what I like anyway.

For personal reasons
This is not an explanation
Nor is it a request for permission,
An excuse or an apology
But you like seeing this side of me
Don't you?

For personal reasons
I'll be giving you just enough
To break the norm

Remain mysterious
Keep you interested
And craving more.

XII

Maybe I'm worth it all—
Every risk
Every extra mile
Even if it takes a while.

Maybe I'm worth the effort—
The pleasure
The pain
That feeling you just
Can't quite name.

Maybe I'm worth the potential—
Heartache
Happiness
Head Spinning lovesickness.

I am, I'm worth every bit
Of my own time
And yours,
For the warmth of a love
So unconditional & sure.

XIII

I'm incredibly multifaceted
More than a cut gem,
Though I reflect as much light.

Each side of me is contrasted
More than the seasons,
Though I change just the same.

To witness my entirety is to look at the sun,
To swim in the coldest ocean,
To be somewhere you've never felt safer.

A privilege
A risk
A whole fucking experience.

XIV

DEATH & REBIRTH

I've landed in a void…
Solid ground crumbles beneath me,
My momentum breaks abruptly
As gravity evaporates.

Fate is finely threaded
With weaves of emptiness,
Momentary deaths
That jolt you forward
Onto the next.

Those pockets of potential
An infinite expanse,
Unconfined to any roadway
Before finding a new path.

Tears fall
For the losses
And for fear of
The unknown,
Before floating up & outward
Like drifting seeds
Looking for a home.

Beginnings only come
From inevitable ends.

So before I fall into that
Hollowness,
I plant flowers over my old bones
And go forward, unencumbered,
Into a limitless
Abyss.

In the Company of a Goddess

XV

Find me in the flowers
And in the depths of hell
I'll be waiting to entice your demons
And liberate you
So you can bask in the sun
And sin in the shadows.

XVI

I met her in the forest,
At a graveyard in midsummer.
Before I even knew her name
She whispered to me
Through flora & fauna,
Through growth & decay.

I met her in my dreams,
In the maze of a rose garden.
Her ethereal energy
A liberating embrace
Drawing out of me
This sovereignty.

We meet under the moon
And in beams of sunlight.
Queen of death & rebirth,
I learn to deconstruct;
To start over again & again.

XVII

Don't look away—
   Humans play in shades of gray.
Show me your spectrum
So I can give it a safe place
To be deliciously dark.

Stop looking away—
   I want to see your
"Not okay,"
Instead of fractured parts
Of your abstract heart
Your soul
Came to indulge in humanity
In this messy, dynamic
Play of possibility.

So don't look away
From my whole being
In all it's terror & wonder,
So that I can look back
To see your scattered,
Searching pieces
Gravitate together into
What makes you
You.

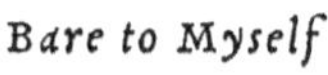

XVIII

KORE DESIRE

I get off on things
That pull on my
Heartstrings.

A part of me craves
That back & forth,
The highs & lows,
The pain & the afterglow.

It's an existential hunger,
A longing to experience
Everything.

XIX

SAY WHEN

I can recognize just how dangerous I am.
I can taste just how you want,
Your favorite flavor.
Look like a dream
With devil wings,
'Cause that's how you like it.

I could be as good or as bad
As your heart desires,
Stick around for a week or a year.
 It still wouldn't be
Enough.

XX

PARADIGM

She tells me she's teaching me
As another wave crashes…
As I receive everything I've asked for
And curse myself for it.

She tells me it's worth it
For the deepest pleasure only accompanies
The most profound pain.
She knows I only learn the hard way
So all my lessons feel fated;
Disguised as something perfect for me.

"But I'm also teaching you,"
She tells me,
"That it won't always be this way."
And she guides me to trust myself
To call back my power
Again & again.
To crumble & grieve,
Then recenter & let the pain wither.

She teaches me through a mirror
Of her own archetype.
To embrace duality
To move with the seasons
To remember I am my own heart

And that I want to be a part
Of this complex & beautiful ~~disaster~~ miracle
That is life.

XXI

VISIONS

I'll run & play
Down that winding path with you,
Opening wider at every turn—
      Surrender
Deeper
Into the dark,
The familiar unknown.

We move, unafraid,
Finding friends
In our monsters
And a safety
In this second home.

We know the darkness
Is as temporary as the light,
The return always comes.

XXII

Did you know that hellfire is blue
And that it doesn't hurt you?
That it feels like liberation,
Not punishment or damnation.
But it *will* burn away
All the parts of you
That aren't true.

XXIII

HIGH PRIESTESS

She holds legacies in her hair,
Memories of lives
That have come & gone,
Trailing down her back
As she walks her own path.

Effortlessly flowing
Between a curtain of darkness & light,
A tart sweetness spilling from her lips
As she sings of a freedom
She found within.

Her heart & mind connect
At the center of her intuition
Where she grows
A glowing garden of flowers
That are free to wither & bloom.

She knows herself fully
And sits firmly in that power.
She can soften into others naturally
Because her own strength & heart
Are radically unbreakable.

From,
The Heart

XXIV

Poems for people
Nearly always drain me dry.
Leave me looking back with pity
And pride
For the art they had become.

Poems for people
Get burned,
Unnamed, reworked.

Poems for people
Will show your naked form.
We reflect ourselves in others;
Parts we'd never directly confront.

My poems for people
Have always come to an end,
And while I hope one day
That this might change,
There's such beauty in impermanence.

XXV

The Devil XV

For 8 years I played a role
Because everything around me
Was telling me I should be happy;
It did much more harm than good.

I was always trying
To take us back to a place
That never existed,
Recreate feelings that were never there.
There was no honeymoon phase,
Even the good memories are laced
With discomfort and uncertainty.
All I can remember from the beginning now
Are tears.

I had this perfect idea in my head
Of how I wanted to feel,
What I wanted it to look like
But that never was and never would
Be us.

XXVI

Resentment Grows Quietly

There was so much shit
I didn't tell you
Just to spare your feelings.
How unfair was that to me?
How untrue.

But now I know
The next time I put another's feelings
Above my own
To reevaluate their intentions.

Fuck you for making me doubt myself
Fuck you for making me feel so trapped
That I go against my intuition
Fuck you for making me feel
Unsafe & comfortable at the same time
Fuck you for manipulating my emotions
Fuck you for making me feel responsible
For your healing & wellbeing
And fuck you
For holding me back for so long.

XXVII

When you lose yourself
In someone else
Freedom ceases to exist,
Your happiness is not really
Your own anymore.

You stop choosing yourself
In big and small ways;
What you want
To wear
To eat
To watch
To think.

You put their needs & desires
Above your own
Over & over
Until your cup is empty—
  Until there are no remnants of
You left.

And when they're gone
You'll feel blank
Like a stock model,
An unfinished mold of a human.

To find yourself—
  Create yourself—

After that
Is defeating
Debilitating
Lonely
And worth it.

XXVIII

THIS IS THE POTENTIAL BREAKUP POEM

If you break my heart
I'll be better for it.
I won't be who I was
Before you.

If you break my heart
I'll be shattered,
Which is exciting
Because then I get to create a new me
From the pieces I find.

If you break my heart
The pain will be unbearable,
But I'll bear it
While I curse your name
And choke on its bitterness.

If you break my heart
I'll pretend like I remember
All these positive things I write
When in reality I'll be drowning.

If you break my heart
I know I'll survive—
      Even if part of me dies—
But I'll wish that I hadn't.

K. Sky

I'm not vulnerable with just anyone,
It's a special privilege.
So if I show you my soul,
If I let you in
Where no one has ever been,
Please don't break my heart.

Please don't break my heart.

XXIX

Your facets match mine—
    Fractured patterns
And shifting colors align;
A dynamic sort of spark
And god does it shine.

I'll let my light dance with yours
To feel our energies combine
And I'll savor this warmth
For as long as our paths intertwine.

K. Sky

XXX

Let me sink into your aura
While I press into your skin.
I want to melt into one another,
Feel the atoms we're composed of
Take each other in.
Let our breathing coincide
Until there's no differentiating
Yours from mine.

I want to take my time
As our minds come
Undone
While our souls
Twist & wind.

XXXI

Wolves

Sometimes manipulators
Are masked as muses;
The art they inspire
Will be bitter, beautiful
And leave tender bruises.

XXXII

BLIND JUDGMENT

I went looking
For meaningless attention…
I was desiccated,
My skin starved.

I had no expectations
I went in blind
Wandered aimlessly
Before stumbling upon you.

Nice
That's what I called you,
But that energy was
So much more.

Instead of empty desire
You gave meaning
To the attention I was seeking,
And I crumbled.

You caught me off guard
Sent my mind reeling
Yet I had never felt so much
Calm
Within the chaos.

XXXIII

A thousand little fires
Lit in the evenings
Rekindled in the mornings
Burning me up and stripping away
My sanity
Easily reignited no matter how much
Time has passed.

XXXIV

Close the door—
      I can't let you in
Anymore.

 No, lock it.
You've lost your access,
I'm throwing away the key.

I'm tired of leaving it cracked
For you to "pop"
In & out
Whenever you please.

When you exit just as quickly,
The hinges creaking,
Echoing in space;
A resonant emptiness.

 I'm not an option or a toy
You can play with when you please.
My presence is a privilege
and yours has been revoked.

XXXV

I wish I could have done for you
What you did for me.
You broke me open,
Taught me how to breathe,
How to see.

You let me be
Everything I needed to be
And when I found myself again,
You let me leave.

XXXVI

What Ifs

If I wasn't so far away & we had each other's hands to hold,
Would things be different?
If we had met a year later after you had some more time,
Would things be different?
If I had played harder to get or hadn't let you in so quick,
Would things be different?
It's unfair to ask and unhealthy to dwell on,
I just can't help but wonder
If things were different, what would we be?
If things were different, do you think it could have been me?

XXXVII

For love, we do very foolish things.
We go to battle for it
With no promise of return.
We forget ourselves in it,
Become pliable so we can fit a mold.
We sacrifice for it
We die for it.

What a maddening feeling,
Loss of control,
Self-preservation cast out the window.
We convince ourselves it hurts
     Until we find some that doesn't—
An exchange of energy that leaves you bare
But feeling fuller than before.

For love, we do very beautiful things.
We break ourselves open
To shine out & let others see in.
We remember ourselves
In ways we never could before.
We sacrifice for it
We die for it.

XXXVIII

Numbness lifted
Like a veil around my heart
The day you arrived.
Flooded with emotions that
Until this moment
Laid dormant inside.

Never have I known
Such unconditional forms
Of joy & love;
The depth of feeling
Unwavering & warm.

If this is all I'll ever feel
      I could die happy—
At least I know for certain
I'm feeling something real.

Moonlit Musings

K. Sky

XXXIX

S ELENE

If the moon could talk
She'd whisper words of encouragement
Because she would still want to hear your stories.

Her voice would be
Gentle and patient,
Exactly like you imagined.

She would call you beautiful
Despite her own radiance,
She thinks you shine.

When the moon talks
To me
She reminds me of her constant presence
Even under the guise of daylight.

She tells me to be aware of my inner world,
The parts of me that are hidden,
To give them attention and kindness.

Her presence feels
Like a waterfall of light,
Like a warm hand on your face.

The moon has secrets,
She keeps you guessing but is consistent.

To her what is right and wrong is subjective
But she errs on the side of justice.

Though the moon can talk
She would still rather
Listen.

XL

If a beam of light
Can travel through time and space,
How far can love go?

XLI

Missing something
That you've never had,
Like the comfort of
Nostalgia
    With no memory attached—
Powerful but fleeting.

XLII

Nothing is permanent
Life is a flow, not a blueprint.
It has no timeline, no schedule.

Find things you love—
        Things you are called to—
Everything else falls into place.

Every single moment can be
Free & beautiful,
Just waiting and wanting
To be experienced exactly as it is.

XLIII

OF THE SUN

I love the way
Natural light plays—
    Reflections of sun rays.

Eclipsed in patterns
Fractured & scattered
Dancing around freely
Unlike matter.

I love playing in beams
It's enthralling, consuming,
Reminiscent of dreams.

It sparks a light within me;
Reminds me I am also
Just luminescent & free
Energy.

XLIV

Pry my chest open,
Show me what I've been missing.
Spell it out inside of me
So I know it's real.

Pull it all out from within me,
It was mine all along.

They say love hurts,
I expect to be broken.
What are you holding back for?

XLV

Just as quickly
As the soft glow of my night lamp
Became an enticing comfort,
It turned into a source
Of longing & desperation.

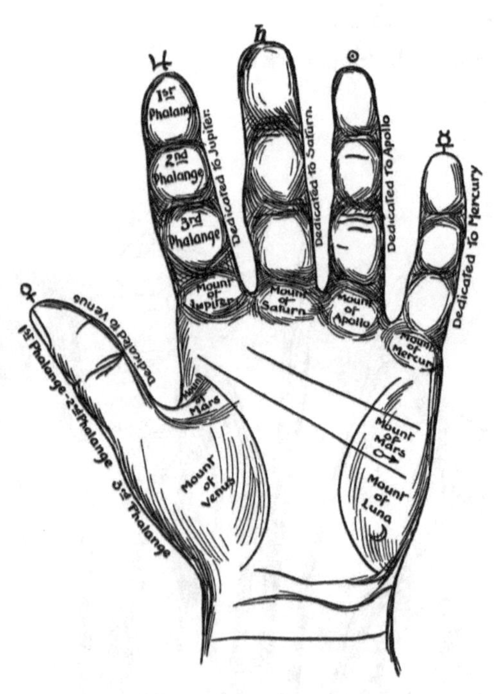

XLVI

There is something to be said
About old poets who knew
That the best verse
Comes from the deepest hurt.

There is something about
Pouring your heart out
Or a visceral rage
Longing to be conveyed.

The same depth of expression
Doesn't seem to come
When I feel content.

XLVII

Just because we've been damaged
Doesn't mean we aren't whole.
Healing can be expansive
But your dents & scars don't diminish
Your worth.
We are human, not objects,
We can exist simultaneously
In pain & in power.

XLVIII

None of us are getting out alive,
What is there to lose if we give in
To the ebb & flow.

Play—

      Stop questioning our every move,
Trust the direction we're headed.

What if it's already enough?
What if you're already doing
Everything right?

What if it's all a lot
More complex & simple
Than we could ever imagine?

XLIX

Dꜰᴀʀ ᴜɴɪᴠᴇʀꜱᴇ,

I'm ready to fall in love…

With myself— my strengths and imperfections. With life, all the little things. With risk and the unknown. With a new city, with new weather and seasons.

I'm ready to fall in love…

With figuring things out on my own, even when I'm feeling alone. With walking down the street and having to stop and tie my shoe. With the most painfully mundane and the most exciting occasions.

I'm ready to fall in love…

With all of the things people find unlovable so that I can find even more gratitude and comfort in everything else. So that the world doesn't feel so unbearable and living is not so daunting.

I think I'm ready for it all because…

Life is worth loving.

L

Swimming in the depths of duality
Soaking in sorrow & joy;
It wells up as gratitude
As grief
As hope.

It's the only way through life I know.

What a strange feeling to describe,
Like existing inside a paradox
All consuming & devoid of control
A powerful pull.

What a beautiful feeling to describe,
Like floating in a liminal space
Where every new possibility
Feels like home.

LI

If you're afraid to admit it
To yourself
It means that you should.

If you can't say it
Write it
If you can't write it—
          Be patient with yourself.

We are reluctant to give life
To certain thoughts & feelings
Because we know how quickly
It can turn something on its head.

If whatever it is can crumble
From admitting one thought,
The walls needed to come down.

So much is waiting for you on the other side of fear.

P.S.

I can't thank you enough for spending this time with me, for holding space for these words and giving them life. Step back into the world and feel, fearlessly. Remember that you are already enough.

With all of my love,
K. Sky